Advance F
The Surviva
Selling Real Estate

M000040623

"I have known Ronda for many years. We met through mutual real estate circles, and she has been such an inspiration and a wonderful resource for my real estate business. She is the "real deal" when it comes to authentic passion for the job and her clients. Her transparency has helped me through so much! I was thrilled when I found out she was starting her journey to write a book and to become a coach. What an amazing opportunity for the rest of us to learn from one of the best in the business! I highly recommend her words of wisdom. . . always sprinkled with love, laughter, and hard truth."

DEE ANN AREY–RE/MAX UNLIMITED

"I have been looking forward to this book! Ronda is not only a true, caring real estate professional, she is an equally impressive person. In several transactions and referrals, I have been fortunate to work with Ronda and learn from her incredible perspective on how we do our business. The Real Estate Support Group social media page has been a gift to our industry, facilitating many transactions and giving us all a place to share ideas and improve our dealings with each other. I can't say enough positive things about Ronda. I am blessed to call her a colleague but more blessed to call her a friend."

SHAWN C. KELLEY–LIV SOTHEBY'S INTERNATIONAL REALTY

"I have known Ronda Courtney for over 18 years. I met her years ago when we worked in the same office. Ronda is not only an excellent realtor who sells a very high volume of real estate but has the great quality of caring. She cares about her clients and other realtors. We have closed transactions together and she is a true professional and her word is her bond. Ronda started a Facebook page for agents that has been invaluable to me. It helps me interact with other agents whether I need a landscaper or agent to refer in another city. It is a wonderful vehicle for my business. Ronda has been a colleague and friend for many years and is what I hope all realtors strive to be. She is a quality person who focuses on helping people and does not concern herself with the monetary side of the business. Ronda is an excellent example and one of the best I have known in my 40-year career in real estate."

MIKE SCHOEN–SCHOEN REALTY

"I knew we were in good hands with Ronda and her team from day one. Her honesty, confidence and sense of humor filled the room and I knew she was special. Every detail was handled as if we were family and when things got a little tough, she got tougher. In a business where trust is paramount, Ronda always let us know she had our back. A genuine person with a heart that never stops caring."

SANDY CLEMENT–OWNER CINDERELLA RANCH

"I met Ronda when I was working in new home sales for a large builder. I immediately had a connection with her so when my husband and I started our own company we trusted her to handle all of our transactions. It has been over ten years and we continue to use Ronda to sell all of our homes."

CHERI DANSKY AND RICHARD MILLS–DANKSY MILLS CUSTOM HOMES

"I appreciate that Ronda has been so completely transparent and real about her own experience to address a common problem many of us face upon the climb to financial success. I have left the real estate business a few times because it was consuming me 24/7 until I could find the balance I needed. Her support group on Facebook has been a great resource for so many of us!

DOMINIQUE NICOLE–REALTOR/COACH

"*Ronda is one of a kind, and truly intentional in her work with mentoring other agents. Her guidance and the other agents I have met through the real estate support group has been an integral part of helping me with my business.*"

AMY RADIC- EXP REALTY

"*Ronda takes readers on a vivid and hilarious read through the ups and downs of real estate. It is no wonder that her social media Real Estate Support Page includes members that are the best in the business, as she mentors them through her down to earth approach!*"

DEBORAH WINWARD–RE/MAX ALLIANCE

"*I really enjoyed Ronda's book. Being in real estate myself, for many years, she hit the nail on the head about this business. She put in writing what the rest of us are thinking. She is an inspiration to me by being so real and authentic. I hope everyone reads this book. It put things in perspective for me and made me realize that life is precious. Work hard-play harder and never take life for granted. Thank you for making me realize that.*"

DEBBIE LEITERITZ–BROKERS GUILD

The Survival Guide to Selling Real Estate

*Release the **Golden Handcuffs** by Finding True Work-Life Balance*

Robin,
Great meeting you!
What doesn't Kill us
makes us Stronger.
Enjoy -
xoxo - Ronda

Ronda Courtney

SRE Press
Denver, Colorado

The Survival Guide to Selling Real Estate:
Release the Golden Handcuffs by Finding True Work-Life Balance
Ronda Courtney

Copyright © 2020 by Ronda Courtney

ISBN: 978-1-7341250-0-9 paperback
ISBN: 978-1-7341250-23 eBook
Library of Congress Control Number: 2019915729

Book Design by Bob Schram, Bookends Design
www.bookendsdesign.com

First Edition
Printed in the United States of America

SRE Press
Denver, Colorado
surviving.realestate
rondacourtney08@gmail.com

DEDICATION

To My Grandmother
LOUISE
1929-2018

Who always believed in me.
She knew this book was in the works,
and while she never got to read it,
she inspired me to never give up.

ACKNOWLEDGMENTS

T O MY MOM, who taught me to be with a man because you want to be not because you need to be. To my girlfriends, for standing by me in my darkest days. To my dad, who always thought I was the best no matter what, and second mom Ree Ree for always just being wonderful! To my brother Steve, who I am always proud of, and my entire family. To Lane Lyon, who helped me write this for three years and Teresa Hoens, Christina Bornstein and Cheri Dansky for helping me pull this off. To Gary Barnes my business coach! You pushed me to get this message out to help others! Can't thank everyone enough.

CONTENTS

FOREWORD

RONDA COURTNEY in *The Survival Guide to Selling Real Estate* has captured the essence, both the positive and the drawbacks of what successful real estate professionals face. She tells her own personal story using humor to offset painful events and takes you on a journey of being a top selling agent to a devastating personal event and back to being on top again. Through this experience Ronda discovers the secret to true success by embracing work life balance. The book will impact everyone in any business who chooses to implement Ronda's process of having it all!

–GARY BARNES, PRESIDENT
www.GaryBarnesInternational.com

Post from Support Page – I modified it to be more politically correct but it is from the Broke Agent who I find hilarious and an asset to the Real Estate Industry.

DOCTOR: Any drugs or alcohol?

AGENT: Yes, I sell Real Estate

DOCTOR: Enough said I will write you a script for drugs that will mix with your alcohol!

PREFACE

Some of the names and locations in here have been changed to protect the innocent and the stupid!

ANYONE WHO HAS WORKED IN REAL ESTATE—whether a dabble or life journey—knows the business is rarely what cable tv junkies see on rich and famous reality shows. The truth is, our jobs include chauffer, a counselor talking clients off cliffs and occasionally a last minute housekeeper. Emotions run high with a home purchase, and for good reason. For many, it's the single largest purchase people make in their lives. For the hard-working men and women facilitating the transaction, the stress can be overwhelming.

Several years ago, I set up a social media page called the Real Estate Support Group. I'd been a top producing agent for almost two decades—but started to struggle. I wanted others to find the support I was looking for at the same time. This closed, private Facebook group quickly grew and the stories flowed out almost as fast as the switch was flipped on the page. It became obvious right away that countless real estate agents deal with many of the same personal and professional struggles. For some, their relationships and health are at risk, and for others, help came too late. In the pages that follow, you will hear these stories of success, failure and rising up again. If you're working in sales, can't find balance and are wondering if or how you'll survive, this book is for you!

CHAPTER 1

The Pond Pump

T HE SPRING SUN HAD BEEN UP FOR HOURS, but darkness surrounded me. I was alone on my bathroom floor. I kept my eyes toward the ceiling as if I could keep the tears from streaming down my face. Out of breath from yelling, the rage seeped from every pore. I held the phone loosely to my ear. "you're going to let this deal die over a lousy $100 pond pump?" I screamed into the phone. Ok, so this was a weak moment. I've been selling homes for about twenty years and won every award imaginable in my company, but that didn't matter right now. I wanted to quit this job and run away from home. The thought of living in my camper and selling fire-wood seemed like a great idea. Afterall I was a great sales-person. I never had to spend money on marketing because I developed a solid referral only real estate business. I prided myself on going above and beyond to help my clients. I treated them as if they were family and never did anything I would not do if I was personally selling or buying that prop-erty. I also worked with them on what they paid in commis-sion. If they were upside down in their home, I gave them a great deal, and in return, they referred me to everyone they knew. I never focused on the money only on them and their situation, yet the money always came.

But on this day, my emotional stability was now hung in the balance, and every sharp-tongued objection from the buyer's agent on the phone was like nails on a chalkboard. This was the second buyer for a troubled listing I could not wait to wash my hands of. The first buyer's financing failed. The next buyer was soon to close the deal, but not without worries about whether an outdoor pond pump was working. This unrelenting real estate agent had no idea the firestorm he was about to unleash. The words flew out with no control. "You are a shitty agent," I screamed. "I effing hate you." (only I went for the real word.) The line went quiet, then beeped to signal the call had terminated. Two hours passed before the cell phone rang again. With a quiet, cautionary tone, Bob asked if I was ok. Bob Miller was my broker; he owned the office and was the supervisor over dozens of independent real estate agents working out of one location. Never had he called with something like this. "I think you need to take some time off", he told me. I knew he was right. I had snapped. Pushed over the edge by a pond pump of all things, and stress from the past six months had built up and spilled over. More like exploded. Bob had warned me years ago working all the time ruined four marriages for him and that I needed to get it under control. I am like most of you, we think we can handle it and nothing bad will ever happen to us. At this point my personal life and the stress of the job was too much for me to handle. My life was stressful. I was completely unprofessional making it almost unbearable.

Working yourself to death and having a mental breakdown is not the way to go!

Questions to Ask Yourself:

- Be honest, do you run your business like a business, or does it run you?
- Do you listen to agents that have been in the business forever when they try and warn you about this business?
- Are you willing to adjust your business model to have a LIFE?

Action Steps:

List three things YOU can change that will give YOU more control over YOUR business.

1. ....

2. ....

3. ....

When a pond pump is literally sending you into a nervous breakdown- YOU NEED A VACATION! Take one!
List the top three destinations for your next vacation.

1. ....

....

2. ....

....

3. ....

....

CHAPTER 2

She'll Get Over It

E VERY HALLOWEEN I HAD A PARTY. It was one of my largest networking events of the year. I invited almost everyone from my world and got a lot of business from it. This Halloween, however, will always haunt me. This party was the highlight of the year for my business. The theme was all wrong but had generated laughs in previous weeks. Guests were told they would be attending a "trashy" costume party. I thought it would be funny and entertaining. Oh, boy!

No one had any idea that by the night's end even Jerry Springer would have been blushing.

As I looked for some friends who had just arrived, one woman caught my eye. "Oh, hi," she said with her fake lashes, cut off jean shorts and flannel red and black shirt. Her name was Bonnie. She was a realtor in my office. We had been friends from work for years. All I could focus on were the little paper dixie cups dangling from her ears. She began talking to my husband Richard (for the sake of this book I will be calling him Dick throughout). He was wearing a mullet wig and a white wife beater t-shirt. He had always been a large support in my business and knew what a big deal this party was for my career. Dick and Dixie Cup had obviously been tossing back whatever cheap booze they could find. He was talking to her loudly in his typical obnoxious way. A wannabe entrepreneur, he had several failed businesses and spent most days at the gym.

As I looked around, I realized I had invited everyone from my world. My neighbors, fellow agents, clients, friends, friends of friends. Everyone was having fun drinking and snacking on the assortment of junk food. I was wearing a white t-shirt with a padded stomach that read "Baby or Burrito," had fake rose tattoos all over me, fishnet tights, shorts and blacked out half my teeth to go with my fake cigarette. I was truly looking my best that night. As I moved to the back yard, much like the front yard, people were everywhere. The stamped stone patio was covered in furniture, a gazebo, fire pit and hot tub which was uncovered in case anyone wanted to use it.

🏠 🏠 🏠

I found myself laughing and blowing off steam. As conversations swirled around me, I noticed people in the hot tub. Only shadows could be seen and appeared to be moving and touching. As I sat next to my good friend, Lane, wearing an 80s costume, because there is absolutely nothing trashy about this man, he looked at me with complete horror on his face and said, "Is that Dick in the hot tub?". Unable to see in the dark, I got up and made a beeline for the hot tub. What I found astronomically changed my world as I knew it. The touching shadows were my husband and Dixie Cup full on making out in the hot tub. Stoically I stood as my life flashed before my eyes. I could have won an academy award for the restraint I exhibited! I was so shocked and humiliated but did not want to cause more of a scene. I felt so much rage that I wanted to kill them both. I envisioned a hairdryer or better yet a TV falling from the sky into the hot tub. Unfortunately, that is not what happened. Instead, I approached the hot tub, looked at the Dick and calmly said, "I want a divorce"! I then looked at Dixie Cup and said, "YOU need to leave"! A crowd gathered with mouths wide open as they continued to witness this train wreck. Dixie Cup then offered a pathetic apology and muttered, "You look mad." Dick's response was, "Don't worry about it. She will get over it." His head was tilted upwards with a smirk that I wanted to slap right off his face. She'll get over it?!?! Those four little words said so much and was ultimately the end of our marriage. At that moment, I could only think of the sacrifices I had made for a man that was never worth it. I had helped him raise his three children, worked my ass off in real estate, and wasted all those years. How could he humiliate me this way in front of everyone? I had recently just bought him a top of the line surf competition boat off the showroom floor. This was our mid-life crisis toy which added to my already huge monthly expenses. I believed couples that played together stayed together and this was my last-ditch effort to save my miserable marriage. Dick really wanted this boat and I sacrificed my happiness to get him what he wanted. The price of the boat was more than what some buyers spend on their homes. I had been the breadwinner for years. I begged Dick to step up and help me. He had refused to get a real job forcing me to work all the time. As a result, my resentment toward him grew. He made every excuse in the world for not making money. Purchasing the boat was not my best financial decision. Let's just call it excessive retail therapy.

🛥 🛥 🛥

In order to justify her bad behavior, Dixie Cup began spreading rumors that we were swingers. Once again, my broker had to get involved in my career. As most real estate agents would understand, any successful agent is far too busy and exhausted to participate in that kind of "playground" behavior. First a pond pump and now this. Needless to say, my broker was less than thrilled to have his number one agent a hot mess again.

The next four months were the lowest for me. I decided to soothe my depression with cheeseburgers and diet soda. The truth is, I was ready for a divorce. I felt like a hamster on a wheel—running and running and never getting ahead. Three years prior to the hot tub incident, the IRS seized my bank accounts because Dick had lied to me about paying my business taxes. My family wanted me to divorce him then, but I was so broken and lacking self-esteem, I could not see I deserved better. I was working seven days a week and not running my business like a business. I trusted Dick and gave him full control over my money. I had no idea how much I was saving or spending. I was making a ton of money and he was spending it faster than I could make it. He was a dreamer, but never wanted to work for it. He was into pyramid schemes and any get-rich-quick gimmick. My mom had joked with him at one point asking him if he was supporting another family with all that money.

I could never trust Dick again. I felt like the most stupid woman in the world settling for this. I had to get a divorce. He had the nerve to tell me, "I did not think you were a quitter." Sometimes the game is just not worth playing. For the first time in a long time, I realized I was worth more than this. I would get over it!

Sometimes we can lose our shit but if you keep your shit you will end up full of shit. Then it will explode every-where creating a complete shit storm. We do not want or have the time for that!

Action Steps

When life gets you down do not sabotage yourself by eating cheeseburgers. List three things that you will commit to do weekly to improve your health.

1..

2..

3..

Do not settle in your life. It is short and not worth it. List one thing you can remove from your life to prompt you to move forward.

1..

CHAPTER 3

....

Work, Work, Work

THROUGH IT ALL, I KEPT WORKING. The problem with hard working real estate agents is they rarely are not working. What once took bulky typewriters, office telephones and ink pens, can now all happen in the palm of your hand anytime, anywhere. We can literally work 24/7 and some of us do. One of the luxuries of our business is being mobile. That flexibility to do our jobs on the run is also one of the biggest challenges. If you want to see the biggest example of no work life balance, ask me about the "girls' weekend" I once took with a fellow agent. Let us just call her Karma. From the first steps off the plane to the sidewalk of the Las Vegas strip, Karma had her eyes and head glued to her phone. "Shall we grab a glass of wine over here?" I asked. Karma mouthed the words, "Let me just finish this call." She was plugged in everywhere except the present.

For me, the trip was a big bore and an eye opener on how we miss out on life happening in front of us. We become consumed with the business and believe we need to work all the time to have the life we want. It's that point where we stop running our business and our business literally starts running us. The question is why? Why do some successful real estate agents shift into high gear until their own engine starts to sputter and smoke? For some, it has nothing to do with real estate. It's usually more personal. It's a realization I made after the pond pump disaster. I needed to make a change in my life and learn to let go of the need to always control. I was watching the agents around me doing the same thing and it was terrifying that was my life, too.

I loaded up my two small dogs and pointed my car towards Scottsdale, Arizona for some reflection. As I sat by a pool for a month, letting my team run my business, I determined where my life started to spin out of control. Working seven days a week, the expensive surf boat, past issues with Dick, the lies, the games, the betrayal, the failed businesses, even problems with the IRS. My personal stress was a cancer, and it robbed me of the patience I needed to do my job. I hid from my life by working all the time and putting everyone else's needs before my own. As I pondered over my painful past, I paused. I knew I was not the only one to have caught a spouse cheating. Not the first to get a divorce. Hell, a good chunk of my business was working with divorcing couples. My rock bottom came with an important realization . . . my life was on the brink of disaster much earlier. Real estate just added fuel to the flames already there. In the years leading up to the pond pump breaking point, I was neck deep in business. By working nights and weekends I didn't have to deal with the reality that my homelife was in shambles. I never felt secure in my life. I did everything for everyone else and neglected my needs. I never relaxed and was always filled with anxiety.

Closing three to six houses a month, was I making money? Sure. Were my clients happy and completely unaware of my inner struggle? Sure. Did I truly know why I couldn't slow down? Not then, but in the hot Arizona sun one afternoon the clarity came like the clear blue sky. "Real estate was the perfect escape," I said out loud, as I sat by a pool contemplating the option of a great tan or drowning myself. At the time, I was up and down emotionally. I was used to being so busy I never dealt with my pain or emotions. Focusing on making everyone else happy and solving their problems. I had no idea how to deal with my own.

My doctor had asked me if I was suicidal. I wasn't because I would never do that to my family. Instead, I told her I thought I was more homicidal. I didn't want Dick to live. I know that sounds terrible to say but keeping it real right? There it was. The "aha" for which I had been searching. I realized more clearly that burying myself in work kept me from dealing with my own issues. In fact, my marriage had slipped away years ago and I coped by not coping. Even when I traveled with Dick I was never engaged in conversation. I was the woman sitting at the table at a restaurant with her husband and texting and talking on the phone. The only thing I really focused on were the deals I was closing and how I was getting more business.

In the months that followed, I poured my thoughts and experiences on my Facebook Page, the Real Estate Support Group. This was a forum closed off from public view. At first, only top real estate agents I liked were invited. Between occasional recommendations for plumbers and inspectors, there were more serious discussions. With my own healing of emotional wounds, I had some fresh perspective and started answering the quiet calls for help. Many of the conversations moved offline. A well-known veteran agent messaged me and shared she was burned out and hating the work. Without missing a beat, I asked, "How's your home life?"

The agent paused then replied, "terrible." I explained that was probably why she was working too much. Same story different characters. The question becomes, did the personal problems start before real estate or because of real estate?

One by one, agents started sharing their stories. Another agent, Sally, drummed up the courage to contact me about a similar problem she had—burnout. This agent was making good money, actually, amazing money from closing 100 houses a year. The stress she was under was overwhelming. She was stressed when deals were not coming in fast enough and even more when the business was eating up all her time. Sally told me, "I'm not sure what's going on. What's wrong with me?" I think I surprised her by answering her question with a question. The question I started asking more frequently, "What's your home life like?"

Sure enough, the truth spilled out of the floodgates. Sally confided in me that she suspected her husband was cheating on her and a divorce was on the horizon. Here we go again. My advice caught her a bit off guard. Could she get therapy? Sure, that would help, but the help she really needed was different. To get there, Sally would have to give up some control. I already knew this about her. She had her hands on every document, disclosure, and detail. What she really needed was an assistant or a transaction coordinator. She needed to let go and get her life back. The cost of an assistant or transaction coordinator is minimal when you ask yourself, what is your marriage worth? What is your health worth? I could relate. I saw her dealing with the same misery I dealt with for years. I let myself go because everyone else was more important. Like me, she had to let go of the fear of not having control. She needed to realize that having help would increase her efficiency and happiness.

When we value ourselves, suddenly jumping off a roof top seems less attractive. (I remember when I was married to Dick, numerous times I wanted to swan dive off a building.) When you're not hiding behind real estate, the problems at home become clearer. I'm not shy. I'll tell you I've been in every mess imaginable in this business. I hope my story becomes an inspiration for other real estate agents. This is where the work BEHIND the work begins. If I had opened my eyes sooner, I would have seen what was going on in my life. I would not have self-sabotaged all the time.

I've come up with the following survival action tips and had I seen what was really going on, I might have saved my sanity and not gained 20 plus pounds from the cheeseburgers and diet soda diet.

Action Steps

1. List two ways you can put that cell phone away and be present in your life.

....

....

....

....

....

2. Help your clients help you. Let them know you will be "out of pocket" for two hours while you take your dogs on a walk. Fresh air always helps! What are two things you can do to make this happen?

....

....

....

....

....

3. If you "work all the time" ask yourself why. Is it because you are too busy or is this an escape from your life?

....

....

....

....

....

4. Put the fire out. What is it going to take to get you out of the flames? Is it surrendering and getting help? Do you need a partner, transaction coordinator or a buyer's agent?

....

....

....

....

....

5. Who can you add to your team now that will increase your productivity, efficiency and give you time to enjoy the lifestyle you want?

....

....

....

....

....

CHAPTER 4

Seller from HELL

DICK HAD GOTTEN ME INTO A HUGE AMOUNT OF DEBT. He had run up every credit card and put me in a financial mess. I owed the IRS more money than I would ever like to admit. I now had to sell my house to pay off all the debt. To say I was bitter would be an understatement. I finally understood why my sellers were so emotional and difficult to work with during divorce.

Selling my own home was the most difficult transaction of my career. I sold hundreds of houses, and yet, could not seem to sell my own. I was faced with the reality that I was selling my home to get out of my debt and my life, as I knew it, would never be the same. I did not sleep for three weeks, resulting in flat out crazy behavior. I kicked Dick out of the house, and he was living with his son. One night I decided to pack everything he owned in black trash bags. The lack of sleep also led me to the decision to put all the framed photographs of us on top of the bags. The next morning, I drove over to his son's house and threw everything he owned on the street, crying hysterically as the glass shattered on everything he owned. As he ran out to investigate the commotion, the hysteria continued as I took pictures when he began the process of recovering his items from the street. Later that day, I crawled into my bed because I simply could not stay awake any longer. I had no desire to get out of bed ever again. The lack of sleep and the anger had taken a huge toll and let's just say I had completely lost my mind. Upon hearing of my antics and current lack of motivation my friend, Susan, one of the top agents in the Chicago area, was very concerned about me and knew I would never get my house ready in my current condition. She quickly flew in to help me, actually rescue me. This incredible friend got me out of bed, staged my house and packed me for the move. I was depressed and consumed by my misery, but thankful that I had one of my best friends there when I needed her the most.

Selling my own house was a no-brainer. However, it was on the market for one week and I turned down a full price offer. I did not like the other company because of past dealings and practices with which I did not agree. In addition, my broker was receiving several complaints about my unfiltered comments to anyone that called to inquire about my house. He strongly advised that I have another agent represent me. I listened to my broker and called my friend, Kim.

Kim has been in the business longer than me and people often made comments that we looked like sisters. She is an incredible agent and probably the only one that could have handled me as a seller. We received another offer from a new agent in the business. Kim had warned her I was devastated by the fact I was selling my house. The new agent did not take her advice and submitted an inspection request list that Kim knew would send me over the edge. This agent asked for a radon mitigation system to be installed when the results were lower than the EPA standard to remediate. I told Kim I was not doing anything and if the buyers wanted mitigation they should go to my basement and breathe because the radon level was lower there than outside. They wanted my custom railings tightened so their kids were safer. They could not be tightened any further because they were anchored in expensive wood. At this point, I did not want them buying my house. I used to think my sellers were crazy when they cared about who was buying their home or when they would kill a deal over a seemingly small issue. For the first time, I got it. It is emotional. This is your home where you made a ton of memories. I understood now why they think the home is worth more than it is. All I could think about was how I purchased this home. I found this great house through a builder and put earnest money down without even consulting Dick. I threw myself into decorating and upgrading because it was the only thing that made me happy. Everything I purchased was custom for this house.

Kim was finally able to talk some sense into me and make me see that holding on to this house was only hurting me. She got this "seller from hell" under control. The experience of selling my home has made me a better agent. I now have more compassion for my clients with a first-hand experience of how they feel emotionally, which makes me better equipped to help them understand the business side of the transaction.

The hot tub was included in the house sale. Hope they had enough chlorine.

Action Steps

List three experiences that will make you a better agent.

....

....

....

....

....

Don't Go!

CHAPTER 5

The Mayor

A S THE SOCIAL SUPPORT PAGE STARTED to take on a modern day "Dear Abby" tone, the stories became more serious. The stress of real estate was taking a physical toll.

My friend, Deborah, knew an agent who worked all the time and was always stressed out. She died of a heart attack at age sixty. Finding data about whether there is a direct correlation between working in real estate and heart attacks is difficult. However, the CDC has listed real estate as one of the most stressful occupations and there is no question stress can lead to heart attack and stroke. Sadly, I saw it first-hand when my close friend, Brad, died suddenly. At the funeral, my eyes were locked on his grieving wife and two daughters.

I remember shaking my head. "This did not need to happen." In a room with people sniffling and crying, I turned my thoughts to the laughs that brought us together as friends and fellow realtors.

I was newly divorced and looking for a townhome in a place people jokingly called "Alimony Park." I did not find this funny because I almost had to pay alimony. I remember telling my lawyer, if I had to pay Dick, I was going to quit real estate and work at my favorite clothing boutique or go to jail. I wanted to live there because it was a gated community and I did not want to worry about Dick harassing me. I could not find anything for sale in there, so I researched the agents who worked the area and found Brad.

I called him "the mayor" because he knew everyone. He lit up a room by just being there. He sold most of the units in Alimony Park with zero days on the market. I reached out to him for help. We set up a meeting to look at a townhome not yet listed. The minute I met Brad we were instant friends. Brad was a 5'2" ball of energy. He found me a unit so outdated I would have to sink $30,000 in updates before I would even let my dogs live in it. We ended up being neighbors and I fell in love with his entire family. We all looked after each other. His little girls took care of my dogs while I worked and travelled.

After a year or so, I noticed Brad's sparkle starting to fade. It was the stress many real estate agents know all too well. The familiar stress of either not enough business or way too much. Brad was feeling it financially. He was driving for Uber and Lyft because he had not closed a deal in several months. The rumor was, some no-name agent was undercutting him on every deal and taking over Alimony Park. I made Brad part of my daily routine. I desperately tried to get him hired on with my big agent friends to get him leads or a management job.

Then, on a chilly Wednesday night, my phone rang. It was Brad's wife.

She was frantic because no one could get a hold of Brad. He hadn't shown up to pick up their girls from school. His phone was going straight to voicemail. It was not like him at all. I rushed to pick up his wife from work. We called the police and filed a report. Where could he be? He wasn't answering his phone. I remembered he had OnStar in his car. Within minutes, OnStar had his vehicle located and were in communication with the police. Several hours went by and his wife and girls were beside themselves with worry.

About ten o'clock there was a deafening knock at the door. I answered. There stood five police officers and two counselors. Everyone's heart sank. One of the police officers looked at me and asked that I please take the girls out of the house. The other officer proceeded to tell his wife they found Brad in the backseat of his car in a parking lot. He died of a heart attack. I will put this down as one of the worst nights of my life. As the tears fell, I saw my own life flash before my eyes. I remembered my father telling me if I did not stop the stress of my job, I was going to have a heart attack.

The officer told me if they did not want the car towed someone needed to pick it up. It had Brad's wallet and personal items in it. I agreed that night to go get it. I sat in the back of the police car on a freezing cold night behind glass. I could not stop crying. I got to his car and drove it to my house. The police had broken one of the windows while trying to get to him. The glass flew all over me as I drove. My mom managed the dealership where Brad purchased his car. The next day I called my mom and she told me to drive it to the dealership and she would take care of it. His wife's name was not on the car, so my mom had it picked up to ensure the family would never have to see it again. One of his wife's friends and I started a Go Fund me page for all the expenses. Like most agents, Brad was not good with money. He had let his life insurance lapse and cashed the refund check the day that he died. He was living commission check to commission check. He had no real savings or retirement. At the time I didn't either. This was a huge eye opener for me.

On my support page, almost daily I stress we need to be happy and live our lives in the present, but it was never a reality for me until this moment. I never thought something this terrible could happen to me or a friend I loved. It was devasting to think you are here one minute and gone the next. I watched his struggle and my own. I was drowning in my own stress, anxiety, depression and weight gain. The day-to-day grind of this job can be too much at times and we feel the financial part can never be solved. I pictured myself at sixty, retired, on a beach, with a drink not stressing about my next house deal or having to live paycheck to paycheck.

This profession can break you. Real estate gives you the opportunity to make a lot of money, but it can also chain you to work until you literally drop in your tracks. Real estate, no matter how good you are, can kill you or make you extremely unhappy if you do not have a good business plan. The wheels can fall off very quickly and be devasting to you and your family.

At Brad's funeral, I listened to tearful stories from friends and family about how he impacted those around him. I sobbed. I kept wondering if Brad had known it was his last day on earth would he have worried about real estate or money. His death taught me to live my life in the present moment because you just never know when your time is up.

Time does not cost anything, but it is invaluable. You can use it up, but you will never own it. Once it is gone, you cannot get it back.

🏠 🏠 🏠

Life is short. Break the rules. Love truly. Kiss slowly. Laugh uncontrollably. Forgive quickly. Do not regret those things that make you smile. Do not wait until it is too late to tell someone how much you care. Once they are gone, no matter how loud you shout and cry, they cannot hear you anymore.

Action Steps

Live your life today! What are the first three things on your bucket list?

....

....

....

Name who you will share your bucket list with for accountability.

....

....

Pick an item from your list that you can do within the next year.

....

....

What are three things you can do to make you and your family more financially secure so that you can do the items on this list?

....

....

....

CHAPTER 6

Being Over Extended
Limits Your Options in Life

T HERE IS NO DOUBT the measure of success in real estate is how much money is coming through the door. I've heard an agent describe it as an "addiction" to find more business. We all know these salespeople. Before long, they have a new neighborhood, new cars and a new lifestyle. A pricey one. We are concerned about making money to impress people we don't even care about. I often describe selling real estate as the golden handcuffs.

Another reason high producing agents work 'round the clock on overdrive is because they cannot afford otherwise. Their success starts to take over. I always say I would have quit years ago but was stuck because I was so overextended. I had the expensive house, boat, camper, over-the-top retail therapy habit and travelled all the time to escape my miserable life. My friend, Christina, joked by saying she always knew when I was really stressed out because I was dripping in retail therapy. I found a clothing boutique called Cinderella Ranch. The owner used to sell real estate, so she understood my stress and we became instant friends. Sandy would literally pick out my clothes, cut the tags off and I would go about my day looking great and feeling like crap. My philosophy during this time was fake it until you make it.

After Dick quit the car business and decided to go into medical sales, he never made any real money but paid everyone to do everything. He paid people to do the lawn, pick up the dog poop, maintain the hot tub, clean the house and even clean the fish tank. Our monthly bills kept me selling at least four houses per month. Dick also liquidated all our 401k and savings to invest into one of his failed businesses. I had no choice but to run my business like a speeding freight train all the time. I was the breadwinner.

It wasn't until the husband got tossed out and the dust settled that I hired a financial advisor and a CPA. My townhome in Alimony Park was a downsize in space, but also monthly expenses. I went from NEEDING to sell four houses per month to living comfortably with one to two per month. It was a freeing feeling to be able to deal with this job now. Sure, I can sell four homes in a month if I want, but now I pay people to help me.

I gave this advice to my friend Shawn. He took a leap and got a partner like I advised. He was shocked to learn he would have more time and make more money. He was doing what I was, which is exchange money for time. Nowadays, I work about half the time and I'm still highly efficient and successful. I work smarter, not harder, to pay bills. I am never afraid to ask for help. If I do not know the answer, I call some of the top agents in the business and they help me. In return, I help a lot of agents by sharing my experiences.

Oh, and let's talk about bills. I have come to realize most of the agents on the support page have zero clue how much their bills are or how much they need to make. I talked to one agent that was stressed about the lack of time he had in life and his high expenses. When I asked him what his bills were and how much he had to make, he could not tell me. He did not know. When you get your finances under control, you can understand how many deals you need to close. For some top producing agents, it isn't solely the money that keeps them working nonstop, it is the inability to say one word. The word is "NO." From those first hungry days, we programmed ourselves to think we needed to take every deal, work every weekend and put up with every high maintenance client because our future depended on it. Somehow, years and countless clients later, we're still saying "yes" all the time. The truth is, never saying "no" often means never saying "yes" to yourself. When we are blessed with good business, isn't it tough to say "no"?

I decided to take this question to the support page. "In a 100 percent commission job, why don't we learn to say "No"? The statement was baffling to many realtors. The reason realtors don't say no is we NEED to say yes to make money. Right?

I came to realize after listening to the feedback that we are trained to believe this. Some top producing agents tell new agents they MUST work nonstop. This business model is a disaster. I'm calling out all the self-employed "bosses" who have the business but are not ever letting their "employee" take a break. We should be teaching them work life balance. We can't just live for this job and not take care of ourselves. I compare it to being on an airplane. If you don't give yourself oxygen first, how are you supposed to take care of anyone else? The "likes" on the page started going up. I explained that at one time I was financially stressed, and I worked nonstop. Eventually, my anxiety and lack of a personal life brought me to my knees and breaking point. I forgot we work to live not the other way around. Having a handle on your finances is the key to keeping your life balanced. Make balance part of your next business plan. Your spirit and family will thank you. Oh, don't be surprised if the new "getting balanced" catches others off guard. I remember making my friend, Lane's, mouth drop when I turned away a last-minute showing request on a struggling million-dollar listing because . . . I had a Botox appointment. Wait, what? I simply said, "Sorry. I can't do it then." Lane thought I was crazy. Why wasn't I dropping everything? What if this was THE buyer they've been waiting for? The reality is if those buyers are really interested, they would be more flexible. I tell my clients what I have available and we work together to make it a win-win for everyone.

I had a friend for twenty years that I had to cut out of my life because she accused me of being a part-time agent and did not value me or my time. She thought it was terrible that she would have to work with my partners too. She didn't use me on a real estate deal because she was going to save a lot of money by not having an agent. She justified this by making the excuse she felt passed off when my team helped her. She didn't understand my team is highly specialized. I surround myself with partners that are as good or better than me. Bottom line: I no longer let people dictate my life or time or stress me out with their last minute inflexibility.

Chasing money all your life does not make you happy. When you serve others, you will find real joy.

Action Steps

1. Realize that you matter. What are three things you can do today to start feeling better about yourself?

....

....

....

....

....

2. List three things you'll commit to adding to your life (weekly, monthly, quarterly or annually) that will rejuvenate you.?

....

....

....

....

....

CHAPTER 7

When You are a Top Real Estate Agent and You are Doing It Wrong

U NLIKE THE PERFECT PHOTOS that show up on social media many real estate agents have so much more going on behind the scenes that you do not see. I flew to Chicago to support Susan. After she saved me with my house, it was an absolute honor to be able to help her. Susan and I have known each other since our early twenties. We met years ago when we both worked in the hotel business. I always thought we were destined to be friends. She is an amazing, smart, beautiful woman. When Susan called to let me know her father was dying of cancer, I immediately went to her side. Susan's father was being placed in hospice because surgery was no longer an option.

When I arrived, I was amazed how stressful Susan's life had become. She had always been athletic, but like me, had gained about twenty pounds. She had neglected her life and herself. Her $1.3 million dollar home had uncompleted projects that needed attention. Her husband was so busy with their two boys, he never had time to take care of the house or himself. Susan's anxiety with her real estate business and her high bills were a toxin in the house. The tension was obvious. She was on the phone nonstop. She was not present for the boys or herself. I recognized this right away because that used to be me. We went to the hospital to see her Dad on a Sunday evening. The stillness of the room was interrupted by Susan's work stress. A listing agent's ridiculous Sunday 9:00pm deadline had her typing a contract at the last minute. While Susan's Dad laid quietly in his hospital bed, she was on her computer and phone. I could tell the situation was causing her Dad undue anxiety. Susan did not have her phone charger, so she chose to go to her car to charge it. Precious hours were lost on an offer that was ultimately rejected. I kept asking her why she did not have someone that could cover her?

I pleaded with her to get coverage for her business for the next two weeks. I reminded her she would never get this time back with her Dad. I offered support and begged Susan to get off the phone, spend time and engage with her dying father. It brought back memories of the time when my grandmother was dying. I was making the same calls and losing time.

Susan's expensive lifestyle trapped her in a real estate rat race. It was a job she now hated more than anything because of the way she ran it. She made a lot of money, but her monthly expenses were more than what most people make in a year. That 100 percent commission job was slowly killing her. To make matters worse, my overworked friend was always rushed and distracted. She constantly yelled at her kids, and there was no time for her relationship, so her husband had been promoted to roommate status. They were two ships passing in the night. There was no joy in their marriage or home.

So often, overworked, overstressed real estate agents know what to do but do not do it. We tell ourselves, "I'm going to do this for three more years." Then twenty years later, after a divorce, heart attack, brain tumor or cancer we finally understand. I constantly post questions on my support page. What will it take to make us get it? Losing someone we love to show us life is too short? Our business can be incredibly fulfilling, but it can also take its toll. That is why my mission is to help people remember what it is in life that is truly important.

No job is worth sacrificing your life or relationships.

Action Steps

Identify a partner or agents that are willing to cover you so you can handle what you need to without distraction.

....

....

....

....

....

....

....

....

....

Don't just be there physically—Be there mentally also! Get off the phone! You can never get this time back!

CHAPTER 8

Success Story

BURNOUT IS OFTEN THE BREAKING POINT for real estate agents. It may be that a life or death situation is the wakeup call that forces balance. I spent the bulk of my career working every lead, every deal for months and months. When I could not take it anymore, I would escape. One hot summer, I checked out. My best friend Julie sent me a plane ticket to visit her in Oklahoma. Julie and I have been friends since college. I jokingly remind her that we will always be friends because she knows way too much. I was at the airport when my phone rang. It was Paul.

Paul was not only one of the top agents in the state, but a long-time friend. We were in the food industry before I got into real estate. He is one of my favorite people because like me he cares more about people than money. I would describe Paul as a good-looking man, however, he weighed over 400 pounds. We have always shared the philosophy that if you do what is right and focus on people, the money will come. Paul had called to tell me I had to quit working all the time and needed to take time out for myself.

Paul had his own story of survival. Several years earlier, a cancerous brain tumor nearly killed him. He was convinced it was due to the stress of the job and constant cell phone use. This experience changed his life and he wanted me to realize changing my ways would lead me to the light at the end of a very dark tunnel. After watching him change his life, I realized I could do it, too. I was watching him enjoy his life while still selling a lot of homes. From that day forward, I believed making changes in my business could save my life.

I started referring my buyers out to my partners, hired a company to install signs and paid people to do the things I did not want to do. This is when I began to give up control. I hired a transaction coordinator to manage all the dates and deadlines and do all the paperwork. I was so inspired by Paul's ability to overcome his medical and personal challenges and decided to take his advice.

When his first wife left him while he was struggling with cancer, he began to focus on himself. He made himself a priority. Paul implemented the team process with his clients. They embraced the concept because this business model achieved greater and successful results. He has an amazing business partner, assistant and incredible team. They cover for each other and make sure communication is key with the clients and each other. This business model freed up his time so he could begin to exercise daily. At times, he found he was able to work-out three times a day. He lost over 250 pounds and remarried. While Paul was in the hospital for over two months, his partner and team ran his business. He still got paid on his deals and they took care of each other like they were a family. Paul's success comes from surrounding himself with people that share his same values and work ethic. The key is finding the right people.

I joke with him that his new wife is smoking hot. She is. I encourage him to write his own book about his weight loss journey. He is an inspiration to all of us on the support page. He is always willing to help other agents be successful in the industry. I am proud to call him my friend. Paul's greatest advice is life is too short to work with clients and agents that are negative. Sometimes you need to tell people, "Sorry. I can't help you," and continue on to the next client who will value the experience you have as a professional.

Learning to say NO to people that do not value you allows you to say YES to the people that do.

Action Steps

Always believe that your life will get better! Help other agents when they need it and be an inspiration to others!

Who do you want to add to your inner circle to improve your life? Be specific!

....

....

....

....

....

....

....

....

....

CHAPTER 9

I Think I Will Sell Real Estate

"I LOVE PEOPLE AND I REALLY LIKE TO LOOK AT HOUSES, so I think I will sell real estate." It's something we all too often hear from people who want to jump into this business. After all, it's days full of touring beautiful homes and driving fancy cars. Right? Sadly, for some agents, even the best of them, selling real estate can cure your love for people and looking at houses.

The "non" glamorous side of real estate is rarely portrayed on those sexy HGTV selling shows. Trust me, I've done it all. I've shoveled sidewalks of vacant listings to ensure showings can happen. I've played counselor when husbands and wives can't live with each other anymore. I also saved a life. Literally.

Shortly after arriving at a listing appointment a potential seller said she was not feeling well. An agent who came with me suggested she lie down. Due to the fact she was slurring her words, I knew something was wrong. I instructed the agent to stay with her children while I drove her to the hospital. She was having a stroke and we got to the hospital just in time. Thank goodness! Let's just say we got the listing and the commission was not an issue. I have signed paperwork from the hospital as one of my clients was giving birth and I sold a house from jail when one of my clients got his fourth

DUI. He had to sell his house because he was going to be gone for quite some time. There was a story on my support page about an agent who answered her cell phone for a client as the agent was walking down the aisle. These are only a few examples of the escapades we encounter in this business.

Of course, the daily stresses can sometimes be too much. I recall meeting a woman who quit selling real estate and now is in vodka sales. She sold real estate for ten years and quit to sell liquor because she did not like the person she was while she was selling houses. Not to discourage any of you thinking about getting into the business. After all, we appear to make a ton of money and live a fabulous life. What you do not see are the countless hours we work and the money we spend to make a living.

Oh, do I have stories. From a seller threatening to beat up his buyer, millennials fighting with me over text messaging, restraining orders, husbands bringing new girlfriends to the closing table. I have seen it all. What I have learned, post meltdown, is nine times out of ten when we put ourselves in their shoes, you realize they are taking their stress out on you. It may have nothing to do with you. Just realize you need to put it into perspective.

To be successful in real estate be prepared to grow thick skin. I have a realtor friend, Anne, who went to a hairdresser for years. Anne had shown the hairdresser over thirty houses. When Anne's father-in-law died, I offered to show houses for her. Instead of the hairdresser calling me, she cut Anne out of the deal and purchased a home directly from the listing agent. The hairdresser did not realize what she had taken from my friend. Not only did she waste countless hours of her time, Anne ended up working for free. Anne cut the hairdresser out of her life immediately.

The egos and the bad agents in this business can also be difficult to deal with. I laugh at buyer's agents that are rude

to me. As the representative for the seller, their rudeness ultimately impacts any potential deal. They are hurting their
buyer when they behave this way. When clients or agents
working the other side of a deal lash out, ask yourself, is this
really your problem. It could be all about their stress level
and it is up to you to not take their stress as your own.

I like it when I have a great agent on the other side of
my deals. It makes selling real estate much more enjoyable.
I once had an agent call to tell me she had good news and
bad news. I like to focus on the positive, so I asked for the
good. The agent said the good news was the buyers were still
going to purchase the house. The bad news was my seller had
held them all at gunpoint during the inspection. Oh, boy!
Sadly, this seller suffered from PTSD, so when the inspector
set off the smoke alarm to test it, he panicked. I calmly asked
the agent would the nervous inspector and buyers be pressing
charges? The agent said at this point she was pretty sure the
buyers would be taking the house as is and would not be asking for any repairs. I felt like we dodged a bullet with no calls
to the cops.

**Sometimes life is happy. Sometimes life is rough. There
is always a lesson to be learned that will make you stronger.**

Action Steps

Do not be overly aggressive. Check your ego at the door.
List five things in this business that BUG you the most?

1...

....

....

2...

....

....

3...

....

....

4...

....

....

5...

....

....

My Suggestions

Communicate with other agents respectfully. You can have fun if you and the other agent have the same goal. The goal is to get to closing.

Negotiate up front the timing of deadlines. No deadlines after 6:00pm. No Sunday deadlines. Set the pace. I discuss this with all parties, so the deal will go smoothly from the beginning.

How can you handle your deadlines better so that you and your clients can have a life?

....

....

....

....

....

....

....

....

....

CHAPTER 10

Get a Life!

W E BELIEVE BEING AVAILABLE TO OUR CLIENTS 24/7 makes us look better. We all want to provide good service and make sure our clients feel valued. However, sometimes the very people we want to flatter, are not impressed with our unbalanced lifestyle. Our clients often wonder why we do not make time for our families. Not answering the phone because you're at Back to School Night is acceptable. One agent told me recently he had to work all the time because he could never give up control. I hear this from countless agents. Same old story about why they put real estate before themselves and their families. I also hear this same thing from top lenders. Are you going to wait until you get a brain tumor like Paul or a melt down over a nasty divorce and pond pump before you look at your life? Is all that money you are making worth it? Do you want to live your life this way?

My phone is on silent all the time. I want to hear what clients need before I call them back. My voicemail states, "For a faster response text me at this number." I do not like talking on the phone rehashing the same thing over again. Instead, I want to get to the point! Most of my support group posts are from seasoned agents that are unhappy because they work all the time. I have said repeatedly, if they cannot let go of their control issues, they will continue to live an

unbalanced and unhealthy lifestyle. My standard response
is "You are good at this job. You have been doing it forever."
Be efficient. Enjoy life. You have this!

Action Steps

Develop boundaries for your business. People will respect
you more if you are not at their beck and call. What kind
of boundaries can you set in your business?

....

....

....

....

....

....

....

....

....

....

....

....

....

....

....

....

....

....

....

....

....

....

....

Take a time management class. You are not open for business 24 hours a day!

CHAPTER 11

HOW TO TAKE A VACATION
—and Yes You Can!

T HEY SAY, AND IT IS TRUE, if you want to get busy in real
estate, go on a vacation. It seems like all the buyers on
the fence or a stagnate listing will finally decide to move the
moment you pull out of town. I recently went on a cruise
with another realtor. I lined up two agents to cover my business and contacted all clients about the plan for the week.
The other agent was holed up in a tiny computer lounge with
lousy internet writing offers and was missing out on the fun.
Sound familiar? My friend was trying to "work" remotely.
Why?

I handed him a tall bottle of beer with a lime. "Guess
what?" I said as I leaned back to keep the sun on my face.
"Don't you think your clients will wonder why you're doing
all this from a cruise ship?" I explained something this top
agent already knew. Everyone takes time off. Doctors,
lawyers, teachers all take vacations. "Your clients can work
with the person covering you. They will not die." While he
thought he was being Super Realtor and taking care of everybody from afar, some clients might wonder why he was doing
that. I say, get coverage and get organized before you leave.
It is okay to have someone covering for you. Grab that drink
and realize it will all be there for you when you get home."

I was reminded of that conversation when I received a call from Mary. This buyer's agent was newer in the business and I could tell was insecure in her abilities. She was checking on an offer she had submitted on a listing of mine. There were multiple offers and she kept calling back to inquire about whether her clients should revise their offer. She spoke quietly and sniffled a lot. I finally asked her what she was doing. The quiet but aggressive agent was negotiating a contract from her mother's funeral! I assured her that I was presenting her offer and paying respect to her mother was way more important. We ended up getting the deal done. I often wonder what her clients thought. She needed a backup plan.

I need a vacation or better yet a new job on a beach somewhere!

Action Steps

Look at your calendar and schedule a three-day vacation. Pick a date and write down what you are going to do.

....

....

....

....

....

Take a vacation in a remote place where you can't get any cell service! Get it on your calendar now. Where are you going?? Get excited!!

CHAPTER 12

A Call for Help

T HERE ARE SHOWING ASSISTANTS, transaction coordina-
tors and buyer's agents. Why don't we utilize the help
when we need it most? I believe we do not want to pay for
that investment. REALLY? What you are basically saying is
"I AM TOO CHEAP TO HAVE A LIFE." I'm fortunate to
have a strong referral business. That happens after years in
the business. Nowadays, I refer out every single buyer to two
buyer's agents. We are not an official team but operate like
one. I joke about how I would rather give CPR to a dead
mouse than show homes. I much prefer to work on the listing
side. I train agents on the support page to do what they are
good at and hire help with what they are not. I must admit,
I can price a house almost to the exact number for which it
will sell and appraise. I'm a good listing agent. I'm great at
staging houses. I have a rock star photographer resulting in
moving these homes faster. On the buy side, it's a different
story. My buyer's agents, Laura and Elaine, do a better job. I
have zero patience. When clients don't like the house, I'm
ready to say, "Let's go then. Chop, chop. Why are we wasting
time?" An agent recently challenged me on this, saying she
could not refer her buyers out because they only wanted to
work with her. After all, they hired her and maybe they do
not want her buyer's agent. I looked at her and asked, "Do

they REALLY care most about working with you or could it be that their main priority is getting into the house for the right price"?

I believe in referring clients without clients feeling "passed off." I tell the buyers that I'm involved, but Laura specializes on the buy side and will be showing them the houses. They actually appreciate it. I do the listing side and Laura handles the buy. We are highly efficient. I can work less than thirty hours a week and close forty or more homes a year. I have learned to let go of many things, such as, over-extending myself, being a control freak about a transaction, and endless other factors that cause us undue stress. I believed every client and everybody in my life was more important than I was! My advice on the support page on how to get a life is "get a partner or a buyer's agent and pay them really well and they will always want to work with and support you." Laura has been with me for nearly nine years. Elaine works with us as a backup and we can always depend on her. I surround myself with agents that share my same philosophy. They focus on being great to clients and treating them as if they were family, while also setting boundaries and parameters. We have a life and we treat real estate as a business.

Do not allow others to take advantage of or disrespect you.

Action Steps:

You deserve to be happy. Believe in yourself.
List ten things that make you happy. (If more than four of them are connected to your business, think "balance.")

1...

2...

3...

4...

5...

6...

7...

8...

9...

10...

CHAPTER 13

Smartest Clients in the World

A NOTHER STRESS FACTOR IN OUR BUSINESS is often times the client claims to know more than you.

I often wonder why a client hires us to begin with if they know so much about selling homes. When the seller insists on doing it their way, they almost always lose money. They believe because they spent $50,000 in unnecessary upgrades with the builder, their home is worth $100,000 more than the comparables in the neighborhood. We have all been there. A client may have sold two houses in their life, while we sold two this month. I am squarely focused on gaining trust with my clients. I have many contacts with plumbers, electricians, HVAC techs, roofers and just about any other home maintenance referral you can imagine. I can read the inspection and tell you exactly what it will cost to fix it. I've also saved my clients huge amounts of money by knowing who to call to fix things. I attribute my success in real estate to surrounding myself with the best in the business. My client can hire whoever they want, but I make sure they are getting the best deal and the best job is getting done. I refer so much business to my contractors, they will do anything to ensure my client's happiness.

Selling a home is very personal. I promote the value I bring to the table when a client threatens to use a discount

broker. I guarantee that they will get the service and the contractors necessary to move smoothly through inspection
time. Sellers need not only assistance in selling their homes,
but also a great deal of compassion.

I think about the time I pulled up to a future listing and
was horrified by the condition. Everyone's idea of clean can
be different, but seriously this one takes the prize! There was
dirty, poop-filled underwear lying all over the floor and a
lovely mousetrap on the counter by the coffee maker. I'm not
joking. Mind you, my mouth filter was broken years ago. The
words just flowed out when I asked if the underwear and the
mousetrap would be included in the sale or if he wanted it as
an exclusion? I ended up helping clean the house, staged it
and my amazing photographer made it look like a million-
dollar model home. You are helping them through a very personal and stressful situation which is also one of their largest
investments. I turn all my clients into friends and have their
back on anything we need to do to get their home sold.

I have learned to fire clients that do not value my serv-
ices, after years of putting up with abuse from buyers and sellers. Simply put, I do not allow clients to rob me of my joy or
happiness. Should you find yourself in a bad situation where
you are not being respected, walk away. Do not allow clients
to make you feel bad about yourself or lose sleep because of
their bad attitude. Rather, spend your time and energy on
clients who are good to you and good for your business.

Laura was working with one of the worst clients on the
planet. This client was an unhappy woman and loved to take
out her misery on everyone. She was selling her house and
Laura was helping her with the purchase of a new one. The
client called me hysterical because during a showing someone had used the restroom and failed to flush the toilet. I
calmly asked her what she wanted me to do. Did she want
me to come over and flush the toilet or would she prefer that

I send a cleaning lady. I also informed her that I could call every agent that wanted to show the house and advise them to not use the restroom at this listing. We could also put up a sign next to the toilet that stated, "Please Flush."

Laura and I ended up sacrificing a chunk of our commission to get her out of a solar panel lease on her new home purchase that she did not want. We wanted her out of our lives. Was it worth it? You bet. I found value in not having Laura show this buyer anymore homes to avoid a mental breakdown. She was one of the rudest women we had ever met. The kicker was when the seller was trying to do her a favor by removing all the old, dirty, lacy curtains, this buyer then requested money to replace the curtains. After all, they were included. Just in the nick of time, Laura was able to stop the agent and seller and have the gross curtains removed from the trash. I must admit It brought me great joy when I called the buyer to give her the good news that we were able to recover and hang the curtains back up for her. The moral to this story is do what you need to do to get out and be happy. Do not play into the drama. I have never seen Laura so miserable with a client and would have paid any amount of money to be done with this deal and see my partner happy again.

Remember: Some of your clients care about your time and boundaries, but others only care about themselves.

Two of my favorite sayings:

"We rise by helping others."

"Be a fountain to people not a drain!"

Action Steps

Some people can be difficult, but you should not take that personally. They might be taking their misery out on you. Do not take a client's stress on as your own. This is not your house!

What kind of clients do you want? An example I work a lot with horse property and land. What would you like to specialize in?

....

....

....

....

....

....

....

....

....

CHAPTER 14

The Cheapest Marketing
On the Planet

NOBODY CAN BELIEVE I SPEND ALMOST NOTHING on marketing to get my business. So what's my secret? It is all past clients and referrals. I think of myself as a networking machine. Everywhere I go, I'm thinking about business opportunities. I sold multiple houses out of my kickboxing club, the owners of all my clothing stores, tanning salon, and massage therapist. Pretty much any business I patronize, I can recruit a client. This enables me to work with clients I like. Some of my clients have bought or sold six or seven houses from me.

I have also found success in selling land and horse property with my partner Cevey. He is a genuine cowboy with a real estate license. He gets all the leads and I handle them. We make a great team. I met Cevey and some of our clients at his ranch to attend a cattle branding. I pulled up in my candy apple red shiny Lexus in white capri pants and sparkly tennis shoes. I did not realize I would be in the dirt watching people hold cows down to brand them. OMG! It was terrible for me and everyone there stopped to ask Cevey who the hell I was. He just laughed and said that's my partner. We sell a ton of homes together. He spent a lot of time convincing our new clients I was the brains behind our operation. I might look city, but I understand how to get their home sold. I love this way of getting business. The internet leads and working with people I do not really know is not my thing and makes me uncomfortable. We all need to find out what works for us and what does not.

In an industry where prospecting for business can take on many forms, I keep it about relationships and rarely work with strangers or people not referred to me. I have taken a call or two from brokers at other companies who call me and offer a market analysis for my own home, not realizing I'm an agent. I told one agent he needed to do his research, or he might as well start selling vacuum cleaners because that is how he was coming across. My mom got a call once from a broker who said she spoke with her three months earlier and was she ready to purchase a home? When my mother said she would be using her daughter, the agent told her she must have spoken to her husband. I wish I could have seen that agent's face when my mom informed her that her husband had been dead for twenty-five years. That must have been an interesting conversation. Find out what works for you, but cold calling with no information is probably not the best business plan.

Do not wear white anything to a horse property. Find good partners in this business. You are Identified with the company you keep. Happiness is an inside job. Do not allow anyone else power over your life.

Action Steps

Understand your clients and their needs.

What do you want your core business to be?

....

....

....

....

What type of property, buyers or sellers do you most enjoy working with?

....

....

....

....

....

....

....

....

....

CHAPTER 15

Surviving Without
Losing Your Mind

As you have read, losing your mind in the name of real estate is a real thing. I am guilty as charged but have learned along the way that you truly can have it all. Yes, it is possible to have a high performing business, make money AND have the life you want. If you can envision that life, you need to start by letting go of the control! Don't be afraid to say NO, hire help and do not overextend. Imagine a world where all agents find common ground. I would love to change the industry and impress upon other realtors the advantages of respecting each other's time and boundaries. It can be done if we all work together. Ultimately, we are all on the same team.

I hope this has been a fun read for you. While I am not exactly proud to admit how it all started, the mega meltdown and the pond pump that lead to a forced vacation, I am happy to be on a path to, hopefully, help real estate agents prevent their own divorce, debt or even death. So, here's to a life of balance, happy clients and maybe a little bit of Botox.

Focus on three things every day that you are grateful for.

ꕔ

I make this part of my daily routine.

ꕔ

I have included a thirty-one page gratitude journal.

Thirty-one Day Gratitude Journal

GRATITUDE

....

....

....

....

....

....

....

....

....

....

....

....

....

....

....

....

....

....

....

....

....

....

....

....

....

GRATITUDE

....

....

....

....

....

....

....

....

....

....

....

....

....

....

....

....

....

....

....

....

....

....

....

....

....

....

....

GRATITUDE

_____

_____

_____

_____

_____

_____

_____

_____

_____

_____

_____

_____

_____

_____

_____

_____

_____

_____

_____

_____

_____

_____

_____

GRATITUDE 4

GRATITUDE 5

GRATITUDE 6

GRATITUDE

....

....

....

....

....

....

....

....

....

....

....

....

....

....

....

....

....

....

....

....

....

....

....

....

....

....

GRATITUDE

....

....

....

....

....

....

....

....

....

....

....

....

....

....

....

....

....

....

....

....

....

....

....

....

....

GRATITUDE

GRATITUDE 10

11 GRATITUDE

GRATITUDE

12

GRATITUDE 13

_____

_____

_____

_____

_____

_____

_____

_____

_____

_____

_____

_____

_____

_____

_____

_____

_____

_____

_____

_____

_____

_____

_____

_____

_____

_____

GRATITUDE

14

GRATITUDE

GRATITUDE 16

GRATITUDE

GRATITUDE 18

GRATITUDE 19

GRATITUDE

GRATITUDE

GRATITUDE

22

GRATITUDE

GRATITUDE

24

GRATITUDE

GRATITUDE

26

GRATITUDE

_____

_____

_____

_____

_____

_____

_____

_____

_____

_____

_____

_____

_____

_____

_____

_____

_____

_____

_____

_____

_____

_____

_____

_____

_____

_____

GRATITUDE

28

GRATITUDE

29

....

....

....

....

....

....

....

....

....

....

....

....

....

....

....

....

....

....

....

....

....

....

....

....

....

....

....

....

GRATITUDE

GRATITUDE

About Ronda Courtney

R ONDA COURTNEY is a graduate of Oklahoma State
University. She has been selling real estate in the
Denver, Colorado and surrounding areas for almost
two decades. She has won numerous awards for her

performance in the industry.
She mentors new agents
and coaches some of the best
agents in the business on
work/life balance. She has
risen to the top of her career,
but has also experienced hit-
ting rock bottom, which has
equipped her to successfully
teach and coach others on their journey. Her goal in life is
to teach other agents to respect themselves and each other
by setting boundaries and exercising time management
skills. She believes life is short and it is important to
live life now!

Ronda Courtney
SURVIVING REAL ESTATE LLC
rondacourtney08@gmail.com
To learn more about mentoring or coaching or to get more
copies of this book visit *surviving.realestate*